Learn to Cook

# Cakes

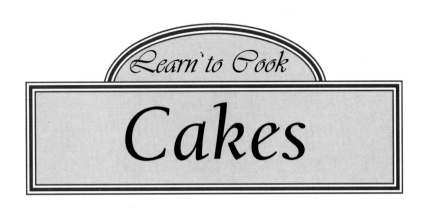

# Learn to Cook

# Cakes

*Janet Marsh Lillie*

**HARLAXTON**

*Double Chocolate Almond Torte (p. 38). Chocolate Devil Cake (p. 19) is baked to make this moist all-chocolate torte. The preparation is shown in the endpapers.*

Published by
Harlaxton Publishing Limited
2 Avenue Road, Grantham, Lincolnshire, NG31 6TA
United Kingdom
A Member of the Weldon International Group of Companies

First Published in 1994

Publisher: Robin Burgess
Project Coordinator: Barbara Beckett
Designer: Rachel Rush
Editor: Alison Leach
Illustrator: Maggie Renvoize
Jacket photographer: Rodney Weidland
Inside photography: Jack Sarafian
Food stylist: Janet Marsh Lillie
Produced by Barbara Beckett Publishing
Colour Separation: G.A. Graphics, Stamford, UK
Printer: Imago, Singapore

British Library Cataloguing-in-Publication data.
A catalogue record for this book is available from the British Library

Title: Learn to Cook, CAKES
ISBN: 1 85837 085 X

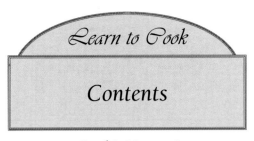

## Contents

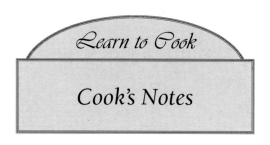

# Cook's Notes

## Measurements

All spoon and cup measurements are level. Standard spoon and cup measures are used in all the recipes. I recommend using a graduated nest of measuring cups: 1 cup, ½ cup, ⅓ cup and ¼ cup. The graduated nest of spoons comprises 1 tablespoon, 1 teaspoon, ½ teaspoon and ¼ teaspoon. For liquids, use a standard litre or imperial pint measuring jug, which also shows cup measurements. As the metric/imperial/US equivalents given are not exact, follow only one system of measurement within the recipe.

An accurate oven is possibly the most important piece of equipment for successful cake baking. Because ovens can lose their calibration, they should be checked every six months to ensure that the temperatures are accurate.

Oven temperatures in this book refer to a fan-assisted oven. Temperatures of these ovens can vary slightly from one manufacturer to another. Read the instructions in your manual so you become familiar with your equipment.

Always remember to preheat the oven to the temperature specified in individual recipes, and position the rack in the lower third of the oven. When cooking in a saucepan, use a moderate heat unless directed otherwise.

## Ingredients

Cake making relies on simple, fresh ingredients to produce good results.

Start with **butter**, if possible use unsalted varieties; **bicarbonate of soda** (baking soda), a fine white powder, plays a role in the rising of some cake mixtures during baking; **cooking or eating chocolate**; **sugars**, including caster (superfine), icing (confectioners' or powdered), brown (soft brown) and raw (natural brown granulated ), golden (corn) syrup; **eggs**, the average size used being size 3/60 g/2 oz; **vanilla essence** (extract); a selection of **spices**, for example ground cinnamon, allspice and nutmeg are the most common; **coffee powder**; **alcohol** such as rum and brandy; **soft cheese** or curd-style cheese; **dried fruits** such as currants, sultanas (golden raisins), apricots and prunes; **glacé** (candied) ginger; **milk** and **plain yoghurt**; single (light) or double (heavy) **creams**; **nuts** of all kinds — almonds, walnuts, hazelnuts and Brazils and finally **flours**, usually self-raising (self-rising) or plain (all-purpose).

*Orange-Nut Torte (p. 37). This beautiful cake is decorated with glazed orange rind, toasted almond flakes and a dusting of icing sugar.*

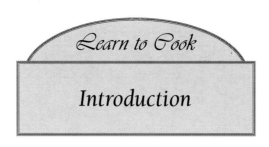

# Introduction

Cakes are one of the most satisfying kitchen achievements. This book provides you with all the techniques, and a selection of delicious cakes to try. They are simple and easy if you follow the step-by-step instructions. Once you have mastered them you can create some of the more complicated tortes and gâteaus in Celebration Cakes; a Honey Cinnamon Roll, as a variation on a Swiss (Jelly) Roll; a Fruit Salad Upside-Down Cake; a layered Jaffa Tiger Cake; a Carnival Cake, rich in glace fruits and Brazil nuts or a classic Chocolate Cake.

Enhance your cakes with toppings, fillings and decorations for a professional look; simply follow the suggestions at the base of each recipe. Some, you will find, require little or no decoration while others, like the Genoese Sponge or Chocolate Devil Cake are made to be layered, filled and covered with delicious buttercreams then decorated with piped rosettes or fruit.

The important information under Cake Basics (p. 8) gives you tips on how to be a successful cake cook, how to line a tin (pan), how to test, cool and store cakes, and how to fill and ice (frost) a cake.

Before you start experimenting, read these basics first and you will quickly become confident.

A glossary of cooking terms is on page 48 for your reference. Be sure to read the information on measurements and ingredients on page 6.

One of the most important things to do when trying a new recipe is to read the recipe very thoroughly before starting. Check that you have all the ingredients, and make an estimate of the amount of time needed. Have you time to make an iced gâteau? Or would it be better to make a simple sponge?

### Equipment

Cake making relies on good equipment—you will need:

An **electric table mixer**: a vital piece of equipment, it enables you to cream butter and sugar mixtures effortlessly to the correct consistency. It beats egg whites and egg white mixtures quickly and easily. As an alternative, use an electric hand beater.

Two **wire racks** for cooling cakes; several **sifters** for flour and cocoa powder; a range of **wooden** and **metal spoons**; small to large **glass mixing bowls**; a **small hand grater for peel**; rubber and plastic **spatulas**; a long, **serrated knife** to level and slice cakes horizontally, and a **flat-bladed** or **palette knife** for smoothing on the icings (frostings) and fillings; a **piping bag** with rose and plain pipes.

A selection of **cake tins (pans)** is essential because the correct size plays an important part in the success of the finished cake. There are many shapes and sizes from which to choose. Avoid using shiny or very dark tins and glass bakeware. Different manufacturers may produce slightly different sizes. For the recipes in this book, you need:

20 x 7.5 cm/8 x 3 inch deep tin (pan)
20 cm/8 inch ring (tube) or square tin (pan)
20 x 4 cm/8 x 1½ inch shallow round tin (pan)
23 cm/9 inch deep tin (pan)
30 x 25 x 2.5 cm/12 x 10 x 1 inch Swiss roll tin (jelly roll pan)
20 x 10 cm/8 x 4 inch loaf tin (pan)
21 x 14 x 7.5 cm/8 x 6 x 3 inch loaf tin (pan)
23 x 7.5 cm/9 x 3 inch (or 23 x 10 cm/9 x 4 inch) loaf tin (pan)
2 baking sheets
22 cm/8½ inch spring-release tin (springform pan)
23 cm/9 inch spring-release tin (springform pan)
24 cm/9½ inch spring-release tin (springform pan)

A **set of scales** is needed for weighing butter, unless you are able to buy packets of butter with weight markings on the side of the wrapper, or can buy it in individually weighed sticks. Use a small sharp knife to cut through the butter at the mark you require. A **food processor** is ideal for quick-mix cakes but unsuitable for creaming mixtures.

## Cake Basics for Success
Read the recipe entirely beforehand.
 Assemble all the ingredients and equipment before proceeding.
 Preheat the oven to the correct temperature.
 Prepare baking tins (pans) as directed before starting.

*Classic Method II (p. 32) preparation. Beating the egg whites at high speed makes firm peaks or curls when the beaters are lifted out.*

Don't allow room temperature ingredients such as butter and eggs to get too warm.

Measure ingredients accurately; do not judge quantities by eye but use scales, measuring cups and spoons. If using, place the cup measure on a flat surface (measuring will be inaccurate if you attempt to hold it) and spoon the dry ingredient lightly into it, levelling off with a flat-bladed knife. Don't shake or tap the cup.

Pre-sift dry ingredients.

Ensure correct creaming of butter and sugar mixtures; add eggs or yolks gradually.

Don't overbeat egg whites.

Take care with folding-in procedures.

Spoon or pour the cake mixture into the prepared cake tin (pan), spread evenly into the corners and smooth the surface.

Check the oven temperature; avoid opening the oven door until at least two-thirds of the way through baking.

Times given for cakes are approximate; the cooking time can vary according to the accuracy of the oven temperature and the position of the oven rack.

Leave the cake in the tin for the specified time before turning it on to a wire rack to cool.

Work quickly once the cake is started—timing is important because once the flour has been moistened, raising (rising) agents start to act.

## Preparing tins (pans)

**Greasing:** Use melted butter or oil. Apply evenly, smoothly and not too thickly, using a pastry brush. Vegetable baking sprays can be used for greasing; apply away from heat sources.

**Lining:** Greaseproof (waxed) paper is the preferred paper for lining tins (pans). Non-stick (bakers') parchment is also available and yields good results, because it is coated; it is not necessary to grease it.

**To line square tins:** Place the tin on a square of greaseproof (waxed) paper, trace around it and cut out the base as marked. Cut a strip of greaseproof paper the same length as the width of the

### Greasing Cake Tins (Pans)

| | | | |
|---|---|---|---|
| *Brush melted butter or oil over entire surface of cake tin (pan).* | *Line tin with greaseproof (waxed) paper.* | *After paper has dried off a bit, dust with flour.* | *Shake off excess flour.* |

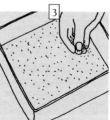
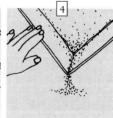

## Lining a Square Tin (Pan)

| *Place tin base on grease-proof (waxed) paper and trace around it.* | *Cut out square to line base. Cut a long strip to line sides.* | *Grease base and sides of tin with melted butter or oil.* | *Press paper in place and grease it.* |

 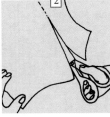  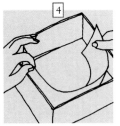

tin and about 1 cm/⅜ inch deeper than the height. Grease the base and sides of the tin with melted butter or oil, applying it with a pastry brush. Place the square of greaseproof paper on the base. Place the long strip of greaseproof around the sides of the tin, pressing it into the sides; grease the base and sides of the paper lining.

**To line round tins:** Place the tin on a square of greaseproof paper, trace around it and cut out the base as marked. Cut a strip of greaseproof paper the same length as the circumference of the tin and about 4 cm/1½ inches deeper than the height. Fold down a cuff about 2.5 cm/1 inch deep on the edge of the strip. Cut the folded cuff diagonally at 2.5 cm/1 inch intervals. Grease the tin with melted butter or oil, applying it with a pastry brush. Place the long strip in the tin with the folded side on the base; press the paper into the base and side of the tin. Place the circle of greaseproof paper on the base; grease the base and side of paper lining.

**To line Swiss roll (jelly roll) tins:** Place the tin on a square of greaseproof paper and trace around it. Measure the depth of the tin, then measure paper from the marked line, and cut all around to 2 cm/¾ inch greater than the depth. Crease the paper along the marked lines and cut the paper to each corner. Grease the tin with melted butter, applying it with a pastry brush. Press the paper down into the base and sides of the tin; grease the paper lining.

**Dusting:** Leave the greased tin or the greased paper to dry off a little before dusting with flour. Use plain (all-purpose) flour, turning the tin to coat the base and sides evenly. Shake off the excess before spooning in the cake mixture. If a recipe calls for the tin to be dusted with coconut or nuts, follow the same procedure.

## Testing if a Cake is Cooked

A cake is cooked when it begins to shrink from the sides of the tin (pan) and is lightly golden on top. If pressed with a finger, it should spring back into shape at once. The exception would be a very rich cake such as a fruit cake which may retain a slight impression and yet still be cooked. As a final check, insert a fine skewer in the centre; it should come out clean, without any moisture.

*Brush the Sacher Torte (p. 38)with warm sieved apricot jam before pouring over the ganache as the finishing touch.*

## Cooling Cakes

A cake is quite fragile when removed from the oven. It is best to leave it in its tin (pan) for the specified time before turning it on to a wire rack to cool. Leave the cake on the wire rack until completely cold.

If a cake appears to be stuck to the tin, run a flat-bladed knife around the sides gently to release it. Paper-lined cakes are easiest to release; as you turn out the cake, use the paper to ease its passage gently. Remove the paper lining immediately. Wire cake racks may also be sprayed with a little vegetable oil or baking spray to prevent warm cakes from sticking to them.

## Slicing Cakes

Always work with completely cooled cakes when decorating, unless the recipe states otherwise. If the cake is even slightly warm, it will be difficult to handle and there is every possibility that it will crack or break when sliced.

Some cakes dome slightly when baked and may need trimming before icing (frosting) to give a better appearance. Use a long, sharp, serrated knife to slice off the dome. Cut only enough cake to give an even surface. Cut with a gentle sawing motion, using your other hand to steady the cake while you slice. Turn the cake over on to the serving plate, base side up, before icing.

Many cakes are cut in half horizontally in one or more layers before they are filled. The easiest way to do this is to mark the midpoint round the side of the cake with cocktail sticks (toothpicks). Use a long, sharp, serrated knife for slicing the cake; use a gently sawing action to cut through. Repeat marking and cutting procedure for each layer.

## Icing (Frosting) and Filling Cakes

To achieve a good finish when icing, turn the cake over so the base side is up. Use a pastry brush to brush off any loose crumbs. Use a flat-bladed knife to spread the icing over the cake for a smooth surface.

To assemble layered cakes, slice horizontally with a serrated knife. Place a small amount of icing or filling on a serving plate to anchor the cake while decorating. Place the first layer on the plate, making sure it is centred. Brush with jam (jelly or conserve) or liquid if required in the recipe, then spread evenly with the specified amount of filling mixture. Spread the filling to within about 5 mm/¼ inch of the cake's edge using a flat-bladed knife or metal spatula. Place the second layer on top and spread with the filling mixture in the same way. Place the final layer, base side up, on the top. Spread a thin layer of cream or icing around the sides and top of the cake to seal in any crumbs and to fill any gaps. To make things easier, dip the knife or spatula into hot water as you spread. Wipe with a clean cloth before continuing.

Spread a final layer of cream or frosting evenly around the sides and then the top of the cake,

### Assembling a Layer Cake

| *Slice cake horizontally with a serrated knife.* | *Place first layer on plate. Spread filling with spatula close to the edge.* | *Place second layer on top. Spread more filling.* | *Place top layer base-side up. Spread cream or icing over top and side.* |

blending at the edges with even strokes. The edges of the cake may be decorated effectively with toasted nuts. Scoop the nuts up in your hand and push them gently into the sides of the cake. Sweep away any loose nuts from the plate with a pastry brush.

## Storing Cakes

As a general guide, you can store most cakes for up to 3 days in an airtight container. Fillings and icings make cakes more perishable.

Fruit cakes can be stored in the refrigerator for up to 2 months, covered with several layers of clingfilm (plastic wrap).

Generally cakes can be successfully frozen, with best results obtained from freezing them in their uniced and unfilled state. To preserve their shape, 'open freeze' by placing the cake on a baking sheet in the freezer, uncovered. When frozen, wrap in clingfilm (plastic wrap) and foil, excluding as much air as possible. Place the cake in a stable container for added protection. It is a good idea to date and label the cake. Store for up to 3 months.

To thaw the cake, loosen the wrapping and leave at room temperature.

## Chocolate

**How to use a piping bag with chocolate.** Extra icing (frosting) or melted chocolate may be scooped into a ready-made piping bag with attached icing tube (tip), using a spatula. With your writing hand, grip the bag at the top with the full end resting in your palm. Use pressure from the palm of your hand to push the icing through the tip. Have a few practice runs first and remember not to fill the bag too full.

Care must be taken when melting chocolate in order to achieve good results. It melts at 40°C/104°F and if heated any higher can burn.

Chop the chocolate into even-sized pieces and place in a heatproof bowl. Place over a pan of simmering water and stir gently until the chocolate has melted. Do not allow a drop of water to fall on the chocolate or it will immediately stiffen and be unworkable for decoration purposes. Allow the chocolate to cool slightly before use.

### Using a Piping Bag with chocolate

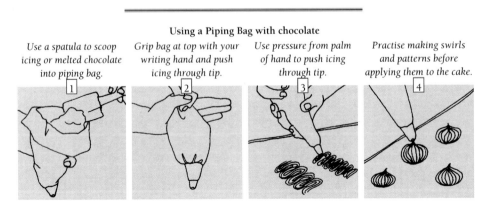

| *Use a spatula to scoop icing or melted chocolate into piping bag.* | *Grip bag at top with your writing hand and push icing through tip.* | *Use pressure from palm of hand to push icing through tip.* | *Practise making swirls and patterns before applying them to the cake.* |

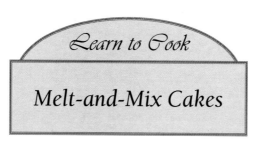

# Melt-and-Mix Cakes

This type of no-fuss cake is ideal for beginners due to its easy preparation and the quick mixing of the ingredients in one bowl. Vegetable oil or melted butter is used with flavourings such as cocoa powder, brown sugar, grated carrot or ground spices. They are simply poured over the dry ingredients and stirred with a wooden spoon or whisked until the ingredients are evenly combined. The secret is not to over-mix. Electric beaters can also be used, especially where the cake mixtures are smooth and do not use grated vegetables or coarsely chopped fruits or nuts.

## Apple Carrot Quickbread

*"All in the one bowl" the combination of flours makes a healthy bread ideal for snacks.*

125 g/4 oz/1 cup wholemeal (wholewheat)
  self-raising (self-rising) flour
125 g/4 oz/1 cup self-raising (self-rising) flour
¼ teaspoon bicarbonate of soda (baking soda)
2 teaspoons ground mixed spice (apple pie space)
225 g/8 oz/1 cup raw sugar

125 ml/4 fl oz/½ cup vegetable oil
4 tablespoons orange juice
2 eggs
2 carrots coarsely grated
1 cooking apple, coarsely grated
1 tablespoon raw sugar, for topping

Prepare a 20 cm/8 inch square cake tin (pan) (p. 10).

Sift the two flours, bicarbonate of soda and mixed spice into a large mixing bowl. Add the sugar. Make a well in the centre (p. 17) and add remaining ingredients. Mix together with a wooden spoon until well combined.

Pour into the prepared tin and sprinkle sugar over the top. Place in the oven for 50 minutes to 1 hour or until a fine skewer inserted in the centre comes out clean but slightly moist.

Leave to stand 5 minutes, turn on to a wire rack and cool completely.
*Makes 10–12 slices.*

**Changing Tin Sizes.** *If you wish to substitute one shape of tin for another, measure the volume of the batter and pour the same amount of water into the tin you intend to use. As long as the water does not come any higher than two-thirds of the way up the tin, you can pour the water out and pour the batter in.*

# Ginger Spice Cake

350 g/12 oz/3 cups self-raising (self-rising) flour
3 teaspoons ground ginger
2 teaspoons ground cinnamon
175 g/6 oz/¾ cup butter
125 g/4 oz/½ cup raw sugar
125 ml/4 fl oz/½ cup golden (corn) syrup

90 g/3 oz/½ cup chopped glacé (candied) ginger
3 eggs
Yoghurt Icing (Frosting) (p. 44) or Lemon Glacé
   Icing (Frosting) (p. 44)
Additional chopped glacé (candied) ginger
   to decorate

Prepare a 21 x 14 x 7.5 cm/8 x 6 x 3 inch loaf tin (pan) (p. 10).

Sift the dry ingredients together into a mixing bowl. Make a well in the centre by pushing out the flour mixture to the edges of the bowl to leave a hole. Melt together the butter, sugar, golden syrup and glacé ginger in a saucepan over a low heat. Cool slightly, then mix in the eggs, one at a time, until well combined. Pour the butter mixture into the well and gradually mix with a wooden spoon, whisk or electric beater gradually until the mixture is well combined, then pour into the prepared tin. Bake in a preheated oven at 180°C/350°F/gas 4 for 1–1¼ hours or until a fine skewer inserted in the centre comes out clean yet slightly moist. Cover the top of the cake with a sheet of foil if it becomes too dark. Leave to stand for 10 minutes. Turn out on to a wire rack and leave to cool completely. Pour or spread choice of icing (frosting) over cake and decorate with chopped glacé ginger.

Makes 12–16 slices

# Walnut Fudge Cake

*A simple, rich chocolate walnut cake that should be enjoyed in thin slices; it is perfect with coffee or as a dessert with whipped cream and raspberries.*

125 g/4 oz/¾ cup soft brown sugar
150 g/5 oz/⅔ cup butter
100 g/3½ oz/3½ squares plain (dark) chocolate
125 ml/4 fl oz/½ cup condensed milk
200 g/7 oz/2¼ cups walnuts, shelled

3 tablespoons single (light) cream
90 g/3 oz/¾ cup self-raising (self-rising) flour
1 egg
Icing (confectioners') sugar, to decorate

Prepare a shallow 20 cm/8 inch round tin (pan) (p. 10).

Place the sugar, butter, chocolate, condensed milk and walnuts in a saucepan. Cook over a low heat until the mixture thickens slightly and the sugar has dissolved.

Remove from the heat, cool slightly, then add the cream, flour and egg. Stir together until well combined. Pour into the prepared tin and bake in a preheated oven at 160°C/325°F/gas 3 for 40–45 minutes. Remove from the oven, leave to cool in the tin, then turn out on to a wire rack. Remove the paper lining, wrap the cake in foil and store until required. Dust with icing sugar.

Makes 12 slices

*Ginger Spice Cake is made by the melt-and-mix method where all the ingredients are folded into the flour and spices.*

### Ginger Spice Cake

| | | | |
|---|---|---|---|
| *Sift the dry ingredients into a mixing bowl.* | *Make a well in the centre by pushing the flour mixture to the edge.* | *Pour melted mixture and eggs into well and mix with wooden spoon.* | *Pour into prepared tin (pan) and bake for 1–1¼ hours.* |

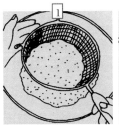  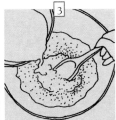 

## Walnut Cheese Bread

300 g/11 oz/2 cups coarsely grated courgettes
   (baby marrows, zucchini)
1 rasher (slice) bacon, rind removed, chopped
100 g/3½ oz/1 cup shelled walnuts, chopped
125 g/4 oz/1 cup grated or shredded Parmesan
   cheese

125 g/4 oz/1 cup self-raising (self-rising) flour
4 tablespoons light olive or vegetable oil
4 eggs
1 white onion, chopped

*17*

Prepare a 23 cm/9 inch x 7.5–10 cm/3–4 inch wide loaf tin (pan) (p. 10).

Squeeze the excess moisture from the courgettes. Fry the bacon and walnuts until the bacon is crisp. Place in a mixing bowl, add the remaining ingredients and stir until well combined. Spoon into the prepared tin and bake in a preheated oven at 180°C/350°F/gas 4 for 50 minutes or until a fine skewer inserted in the centre comes out clean. Remove, cool in the tin for 5 minutes, then turn out on to a wire rack and leave to cool completely.

*Makes 16 slices*

# Carnival Cake

200 g/7 oz/2¼ cups Brazil nuts

90 g/3 oz/½ cup glacé (candied) cherries, halved

150 g/5 oz/1 cup chopped dates

125 g/4 oz/¾ cup raisins

150 g/5 oz/1 cup coarsely chopped glacé (candied) pineapple

90 g/3 oz/½ cup chopped glacé (candied) ginger

125 g/4 oz/1 cup plain (all purpose) flour, sifted

125 g/4 oz/½ cup caster (superfine) sugar

4 eggs, lightly beaten

1 teaspoon ground mixed spice (apple pie spice)

5 tablespoons brandy

Prepare a 20cm/8inch square or ring (tube) tin (pan) (p. 10).

Place 1 cup Brazil nuts in a mixing bowl. Add the remaining ingredients, reserving 3 tablespoons brandy. Stir until mixture is well combined. Spoon into the prepared tin, flatten the surface with a spatula, and press the remaining Brazil nuts on the top. Place in the oven and bake for 1½ hours or until a fine skewer inserted in the centre comes out clean but slightly moist.

Remove from the oven, spoon over the brandy and leave to stand for 10 minutes. Turn out on to a wire rack and leave to cool completely. Wrap in foil and store until required.

*Makes 16 slices.*

*Carnival Cake. Brazil nuts and glacé fruits combined with other ingredients make this easy 'one bowl' cake.*

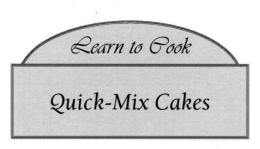

# Learn to Cook

# Quick-Mix Cakes

The reason for these cakes being called quick-mix is that they are made in the bowl of a food processor using the chopping blade. This blade can adapt to the melt-and-mix or rub-in methods found in recipes like Rock Cakes or apple or other fruit shortcakes. If you do not have a food processor, you can use the melt-and-mix technique (p. 15) or simply chop the butter into small pieces and rub it into the sifted dry ingredients with the tips of your fingers, lifting up the flour from the bowl until the mixture has a fine, crumbly texture. The liquid ingredients are combined and mixed in with a flat-bladed knife.

## Chocolate Devil Cake

225 g/8 oz/2 cups self-raising (self-rising) flour
200 g/7 oz/scant 1 cup caster (superfine) sugar
60 g/2 oz/½ cup cocoa powder
1 teaspoon bicarbonate of soda (baking soda)

125 g/4 oz/½ cup butter, melted
250 ml/8 fl oz/1 cup plain yoghurt
2 eggs
1 teaspoon vanilla essence (extract)

Prepare a deep 20 cm/8 inch round tin (pan) (p. 10).

Place the flour, sugar, cocoa powder and bicarbonate of soda in a food processor and blend using the chopping blade for three seconds. Add the butter, yoghurt and eggs. Process until the mixture is smooth and well combined. Pour into the prepared tin and bake in a preheated oven at 180°C/350°F/gas 4 for 50 minutes or until a fine skewer inserted into the centre comes out clean. Leave to stand in the tin for 5 minutes, turn out on to a wire rack and leave to cool completely.
*Serves 8–10*

**Chocolate Devil Cake**

| *Put dry ingredients into the food processor and blend.* | *Add butter, yoghurt and eggs and blend until smooth.* | *Pour mixture into prepared cake tin (pan). Bake for 50 minutes.* | *Leave to stand 5 minutes, then turn on to wire rack to cool.* |

# Apple Shortcake

*The streusel or crumble cinnamon topping adds interest to this warm dessert cake. Ripe cooking pears or drained, canned apricot halves or peach slices could also be used.*

225 g/8 oz/2 cups self-raising (self-rising) flour
125 g/4 oz/½ cup caster (superfine) sugar
125 g/4 oz/½ cup butter, melted
2 eggs
4 tablespoons milk
2 large green cooking apples, peeled, cored and
    cut into thick slices

125 g/4 oz/1 cup shelled walnuts, pecans or
    hazelnuts, coarsely chopped

STREUSEL TOPPING
60 g/2 oz/¼ cup butter
60 g/2 oz/½ cup plain (all-purpose) flour
60 g/2 oz/¼ cup caster (superfine) sugar
1 teaspoon ground cinnamon

Prepare a 23 cm/9 inch spring-release tin (springform pan) (p. 10).

Place the flour in the bowl of a food processor and add the sugar, butter, eggs and milk. Blend using the chopping blade until combined together well. Spread the mixture over the base of the prepared tin. Arrange the apple slices and choice of nuts over the cake mixture pressing them in slightly.

Wash and dry the bowl, blade and lid of the food processor. Combine the Streusel Topping ingredients in the bowl. Pulse using the chopping blade until the mixture resembles coarse breadcrumbs.

Sprinkle the streusel topping over the apples and choice of nuts. Place in the oven and bake for 35–40 minutes or until a fine skewer inserted in the centre comes out clean. Remove, leave to cool for 5 minutes then release the clip and pan sides. Serve warm with whipped cream as a dessert or cold with coffee.

*Serves 6–8*

*Above and left: Apple Shortcake—sliced apple rings and a streusel topping make this easy cake different. A cake to serve as a dessert with cream or plain yoghurt, or as a treat with coffee.*

**How to Separate Eggs.** *Tap the egg lightly on the side of a bowl. Where the egg cracks, pull open the shell. Gently tip the yolk from one side of the shell to the other, being careful not to pierce it (the white will fall from the shell). No yolk must be allowed to fall into the whites in the bowl or they will not beat successfully.*

*Favourite Rock Cakes—a food processor makes these individual walnut and fruit cakes so easily.*

# Rock Cakes

*Fruit, coconut and walnuts combine together with spices and flour to make individual cakes—ideal for a treat.*

225 g/8 oz/2 cups self-raising (self-rising) flour
½ teaspoon ground cinnamon
100 g/3½ oz/7 tablespoons butter, softened,
   cut into small pieces
125 g/4 oz/½ cup caster (superfine) sugar
75 g/2½ oz/½ cup currants

20 g/¾ oz/3 tablespoons desiccated (shredded)
   coconut
60 g/2 oz/½ cup walnuts, roughly chopped
1 egg, lightly beaten
125 ml/4 fl oz/½ cup milk
2 teaspoons vanilla essence (extract)

Prepare two baking sheets and dust with flour (p. 10).

Place all the ingredients in a food processor and pulse, using the chopping blade, until well combined. Place rounded tablespoonfuls of the mixture on the prepared baking sheets, leaving 5 cm/2 inches between each, allowing for the mixture to spread while baking. Sprinkle a little extra sugar over each cake. Place one baking sheet in a preheated oven at 200°C/400°F/gas 6 and bake for 12–15 minutes or until golden brown. Leave to stand on sheet for 5 minutes, then remove on to wire racks to cool. Bake remaining rock cakes as above.

*Makes about 15*

## Learn to Cook

# Classic Cakes and Sponges

There are two classic methods of making cakes which any beginner cook needs to master. The first involves the creaming together of butter and sugar until the mixture is light, virtually white and very creamy, and is referred to in this book as Classic Method I. The resulting cakes are known as butter sponges, Victoria sponges and buttercakes in some countries. Classic Method II refers to the method of beating egg whites until firm peaks form, or yolks until they are pale and thick, then beating in the sugar until it has dissolved and the combined mixture becomes pale yellow and glossy. The sifted flour and other ingredients are then folded in lightly and quickly. Light and airy sponges are the result. Master these two Classic Methods and many variations can be made.

*Classic Method I. (p. 26) preparation. Beating butter and sugar until light and creamy before adding the eggs is an important technique to master.*

### Making Classic Method I

| | | | |
|---|---|---|---|
| Beat butter and sugar in a small bowl until light and creamy. | Beat in eggs, transfer to a large bowl and fold in flour and milk. | Spoon mixture into a prepared tin (pan) and smooth the surface. | Bake. Turn cake out on to a rack to cool. Remove paper lining. |

  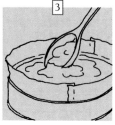 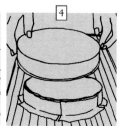

# *Classic Method I*

125 g/4 oz/½ cup butter
175 g/6 oz/¾ cup caster (superfine) sugar
2 eggs, lightly beaten
1 teaspoon vanilla essence (extract)

225 g/8 oz/2 cups self-raising (self-rising) flour, sifted
125 ml/4 fl oz/½ cup milk

Apply melted butter or other shortening to the base and sides of a 20 x 7.5 cm/8 x 3 inch deep cake tin (pan) evenly, using a pastry brush. Line the base with a round of non stick (bakers') parchment or greaseproof (waxed) paper (p. 10) and brush again.

Beat the butter and sugar in a small bowl with an electric beater until the mixture is light and creamy, scraping the sides of the bowl with a spatula several times to make sure the sugar and butter are well combined and there are no traces of sugar granules.

Beat in the eggs gradually, beating thoroughly after each addition. Beat in the vanilla essence. Transfer the mixture to a large bowl. Using a metal spoon, fold in flour gently, alternately with the milk, until it is just combined and almost smooth.

Spoon or pour the mixture into the prepared tin. Spread evenly into the corners and smooth the surface using a spatula. Place in a preheated oven at 180°C/350°F/gas 4 and bake for 40–45 minutes or until a fine skewer inserted in the centre comes out clean.

Leave the cake in the tin for 5 minutes, then turn it out on to a wire rack to cool. Remove the paper lining. Serve plain or spread over with any Buttercream (p. 45) or Glacé (p. 44) icing (frosting).

*Serves 8*

*Overleaf: Top left: Ginger Spice Cake (p. 16) with a glacé icing; bottom left: Carnival Cake (p. 18), an easy-to-store fruit cake; top right: Favourite Rock Cakes (p. 22), a healthy treat; centre right: Génoese (p. 34), a simple gâteau with butter cream and toffee decoration.*

**Variations**

**Orange Cake** Substitute the grated peel of 1 orange and 125 ml/4 fl oz/½ cup orange juice for the milk.

**Nut Spice Cake** Add 1 teaspoon mixed spice (apple-pie spice) and 60 g/2 oz/½ cup finely chopped walnuts or pecan nuts with the flour. Brush the cake while still warm with melted butter and sprinkle over a mixture of 3 tablespoons caster (superfine) sugar and ½ teaspoon mixed spice.

**Chocolate Cake** Sift 60 g/2 oz/½ cup cocoa powder with the flour, and increase the milk to 175 ml/6 fl oz/¾ cup, if mixture is too dry to spoon or pour into the cake tin.

# Rich Fruit Cake

*There are many variations on this favourite rich fruit cake. Once baked it should be stored for at least a month, or longer if time permits, to develop texture. It makes an excellent celebration cake for Christmas or other special occasions.*

*225 g/8 oz/1½ cups raisins*
*500 g/18 oz/3 cups sultanas (golden raisins)*
*125 g/4 oz/¾ cup currants*
*125 g/4 oz/¼ cup mixed citrus peel*
*250 g/9 oz/1½ cups prunes, stoned (pitted) and cut in half*
*60 g/2 oz/⅓ cup blanched almonds*
*225 g/8 oz/2 cups plain (all purpose) flour*

*1 teaspoon mixed spice (apple-pie spice)*
*¼ teaspoon each ground nutmeg, cinnamon and salt*
*250 g/9 oz/generous 1¼ cups butter*
*175 g/6 oz/1 cup soft brown sugar*
*4 eggs*
*1 teaspoon vanilla essence (extract)*
*Additional blanched almonds if liked, to decorate*
*Additional rum or brandy*

Combine the fruit and almonds in a large bowl, mix in the rum or brandy, cover and leave to stand overnight.

Prepare a deep 20 cm/8 inch round tin (pan) (p. 10). Include a layer of brown paper on the base and a double layer of greaseproof (waxed) paper around the sides.

Sift the flour, spices and salt into a bowl. Prepare the cake using the Classic Method I (p. 26), folding the fruit and nut mixture in alternately with the flour. Spoon into the prepared tin and press the additional almonds in to a decorative pattern on top. Wrap a double thickness of brown paper around the outside of the tin and secure with paper clips or pins before baking—this protects and insulates the cake during the long cooking time. Bake in a preheated oven at 150°C/300F°/gas 2 for 3–3½ hours. Remove, sprinkle over the additional rum or brandy and leave to cool in the tin before turning out. Place in an airtight container or wrap in foil.

*Serves 10-12*

# Coconut Ice Cake

*This cake is so moist with the flavour of coconut and soured cream–it will keep successfully for a week.*

2 tablespoons desiccated (shredded) coconut
125 g/4 oz/½ cup butter
200 g/7 oz/scant 1 cup caster (superfine) sugar
2 eggs
175 g/6 oz/1½ cups self-raising (self-rising) flour, sifted

4 tablespoons milk
300 ml/½ pint/1¼ cups soured cream
45 g/1½ oz/½ cup desiccated (shredded) coconut
Coconut Ice Icing (Frosting) (p. 45)
1 teaspoon vanilla essence (extract)

Prepare a deep 23 cm/9 inch round tin (pan) (p. 10) and dust the side with the coconut by turning the tin so it adheres evenly. Prepare the cake using Classic Method I (p. 26), finally folding in the soured cream and coconut. Bake in a preheated oven at 180°C/350°F/gas 4 for 1 hour. Leave the cake in the tin for 5 minutes, then turn it out on to a wire rack to cool. The centre of the cake may be a little wet but it will firm on cooling. Spread over Coconut Ice Icing (Frosting) (p. 45).
*Serves 8*

# Light Fruit Cake

*A light fruit cake which stores well in an airtight container or foil. Toss the fruit mixture in a tablespoon of the flour–this helps in distributing the fruit evenly throughout the cake.*

250 g/9 oz/generous one cup butter
200 g/7 oz/scant 1 cup caster (superfine) sugar
3 eggs, beaten
75 g/2½ oz/½ cup sultanas (golden raisins)
75 g/2½ oz/½ cup currants

45 g/1½ oz/¼ cup mixed citrus peel
275 g/10 oz/2½ cups plain (all-purpose) flour sifted
1 teaspoon baking powder
2 tablespoons milk

Prepare a deep 20 cm/8 inch round tin (pan) (p. 10). Prepare the cake using Classic Method I (p. 26), mixing in the fruit before the flour and baking powder. Bake in a preheated oven at 150°C/300°F/gas 2 for 45 minutes. Leave to stand for 10 minutes, then turn out on to a wire rack to cool.
*Serves 8*

*Coconut Ice Cake. Coconut and soured cream make a delicious variation to Classic Method I.*

# Jaffa Tiger Cake

*It's called a Tiger Cake because of the chocolate and orange layers which are sandwiched together.*

175 g/6 oz/¾ cup butter
200 g/7 oz/scant 1 cup caster (superfine) sugar
3 eggs
225 g/8 oz/2 cups self-raising (self-rising) flour

4 tablespoons single (light) cream
Grated peel of ½ orange
2 tablespoons cocoa powder

Prepare two, 20 x 4 cm/8 x 1½ inch shallow round tins (pans) (p. 10).
Prepare the cake using Classic Method I (p. 26), then spoon half the mixture into another bowl. Fold the orange peel lightly through one half and the cocoa powder through the other, and spoon separately into the two prepared tins. Bake in a preheated oven at 180°C/350°F/gas 4 for 25–30 minutes. Leave to stand for 5 minutes, then turn out on to a wire rack to cool.
Make up No-Fuss Buttercream (p. 46) substituting the grated peel of 1 orange for the vanilla essence (extract). Spread about 6 mm/¼ inch over one cake and press the other cake on top to sandwich together. Spread the remaining Buttercream over the top and sides to cover completely. Decorate with shavings of grated chocolate (p. 47)
*Serves 8*

# Sunflower Banana Bread

*Bananas are always a favourite. Enjoy the flavour in this wholesome health cake made with wholemeal flour and extra bran.*

225 g/8 oz/2 cups wholemeal (wholewheat) self-raising (self-rising) flour
½ teaspoon bicarbonate of soda (baking soda)
2 tablespoons unprocessed bran
60 g/2 oz/¼ cup butter, softened
60 g/2 oz/¼ cup caster (superfine) sugar

250 g/9 oz generous 1 cup smooth ricotta (smooth cottage/curd style) cheese
2 eggs
3 small ripe bananas, mashed
2–3 tablespoons milk
3 tablespoons sunflower seeds

Prepare a 21 x 14 x 7.5 cm/8 x 6 x 3 inch loaf tin (pan) (p. 10). Sift flour and soda together, return the husks and add the bran. Prepare the cake using Classic Method I (p. 26), beating the cheese with the butter and sugar. Spoon into the prepared tin. Sprinkle over sunflower seeds. Bake in a preheated oven at 180°C/350°F/gas 4 for 1 hour or until a fine skewer inserted in the centre comes out clean. Leave to stand for 10 minutes, then turn out on to a wire rack to cool.
*Makes 12–16 slices*

# Chocolate-Orange Baba Cake

*Simple yet moist and rich–the combination of orange and chocolate never goes amiss. A fresh orange syrup and Chocolate Ganache make it an enjoyable special occasion dessert.*

3 oranges

4 eggs

225 g/8 oz/1 cup caster (superfine) sugar

275 ml/9 fl oz/generous 1 cup milk

225 g/8 oz/2 cups self-raising (self-rising) flour

4 tablespoons dark cocoa powder

SYRUP

Juice of 2 oranges

125 g/4 oz/½ cup caster sugar

125 ml/4 fl oz/½ cup brandy

Chocolate Ganache for icing and to decorate (p. 45)

Prepare a 24 cm/9½ inch spring-release tin (springform pan) (p. 10).

Grate the peel finely and squeeze the juice from 2 of the oranges. Cut away the white pith from the remaining orange and leave to stand.

Beat the eggs together in a large bowl using an electric beater until pale yellow and thick.

Add the sugar gradually, beating continuously until dissolved. Fold in the peel and milk. Sift the flour over the mixture and fold in (p. 32). Pour three-quarters of the orange sponge mixture into the prepared tin, fold the cocoa through the remainder and spoon over the top of the mixture in the tin. Place in the oven and bake for 45–50 minutes or until a fine skewer inserted in the centre comes out clean. Remove and leave to stand for 10 minutes.

Place reserved orange juice, sugar and brandy in a saucepan, boil over medium heat until syrup is reduced by half.

Release tin sides and pour over the syrup carefully, allowing it to soak into the cake. Leave to cool completely.

Remove the cake from the tin base and peel away the paper. Place on a wire rack. Cover with a Chocolate Ganache (p. 45). Pipe on 8 or 10 rosettes of chocolate buttercream (p. 45). Cut remaining orange into segments and decorate torte.

*Serves 8–10*

**Crystallized Citrus Peel.** *Cut the peel of 1–2 oranges, lemons or grapefruits, into fine julienne. Drop the peel into boiling water for 2 minutes, then drain. Heat 125 g/4 oz/½ cup caster (superfine) sugar and 3 tablespoons water in a small saucepan and stir until the sugar dissolves. Bring to the boil and simmer without stirring until it becomes translucent and candied in appearance. Add the peel and cook 1–2 minutes. Remove the peel from the syrup and drain on a wire rack. Reserve syrup.*

*Classic Method II. Whipped cream and strawberry jam make a simple filling for sponge layers.*

## Classic Method II

125 g/4 oz/1 cup self-raising (self-rising) flour
4 eggs, separated
125 g/4 oz/½ cup caster (superfine) sugar
150 ml/¼ pint/⅔ cup double (heavy) cream

1 teaspoon vanilla essence (extract)
150 g/5 oz/½ cup strawberry jam (conserve)
Icing (confectioners') sugar, to decorate

**Chocolate.** *Both cooking and eating chocolate are suitable for cake-making. Cooking chocolate is more commonly used as it has a higher vegetable fat content, and a lower amount of cocoa butter. This makes it very easy to melt. Eating chocolate has a higher amount of cocoa butter which gives a richer flavour to cakes like tortes.*

Apply melted butter or oil over the base and sides evenly of two 20 x 4 cm/8 x 1½ inch shallow round tins (pans) using a pastry brush. Line the bases with rounds of greaseproof (waxed) paper, brush again with butter or oil or use non-stick (bakers') parchment. Dust each with a tablespoon of flour, turning each tin to coat the base and sides evenly. Shake off the excess before pouring in the cake mixture.

Sift the flour three times on to paper. Place the egg whites in a clean, dry, small bowl. Beat with an electric beater at high speed until firm peaks form—the whites should hold a firm peak or curl when the beater is lifted out. Add the sugar gradually, beating continuously until it completely dissolves—the mixture should be very thick and glossy when the beater is lifted and should hold straight peaks.

Beat the egg yolks lightly in a separate bowl, then beat them into the white mixture. Transfer to a large bowl. Fold in the flour using a large metal spoon by running the spoon along the bottom of the bowl and up again in one sweeping circular action, then cut down through the centre of the mixture on the next fold, turning the bowl as you fold. Repeat these actions until the ingredients are combined.

Pour the mixture evenly between the two tins. Bake in a preheated oven at 180°C/350°F/gas 4 for 20 minutes until the sponges are a pale golden colour and shrink slightly from the sides.

Leave to stand for 5 minutes, then turn out on to wire racks to cool completely. Peel away the paper linings.

Beat together the cream and vanilla essence in a bowl until it forms firm peaks. Spread jam over both sponge layers, using a flat spatula, then spoon the vanilla cream onto the centre of one of the layers and spread out carefully to within 5 mm/¼ inch of the rim. Place the other layer on top, pressing down lightly, and sift a light layer of icing sugar over the top.

*Serves 8*

### Classic Method II

| | | | |
|---|---|---|---|
| *Beat egg whites until firm peaks form when beaters are lifted out.* | *After adding sugar and egg yolks, transfer to larger bowl. Fold in flour.* | *Pour mixture evenly into 2 lined tins (pans). Bake for 20 minutes.* | *Spread jam and cream between layers. Sift icing (confectioner's) sugar over cake.* |

# Génoese Sponge

*This fine textured sponge mixture is more specialised but the result is well worthwhile.*
*The whole eggs and sugar are beaten over simmering water until very pale yellow and thick, then removed from the*
*heat, beaten until almost double in volume before the dry ingredients are folded in. When baked and cool, it is used*
*for the preparation of both simple and elaborate gâteaux.*

125 g/4 oz/1 cup self-raising (self-rising) flour
4 eggs, lightly beaten
90 g/3 oz/scant ⅓ cup caster (superfine) sugar

60 g/2 oz/¼ cup butter, melted
2 teaspoons vanilla essence (extract)

Prepare a 20 cm/8 inch x 7.5 cm/3 inch round tin (pan) (p. 10).

Sift the flour twice. Combine the eggs and sugar in a heatproof bowl. Place it over a pan of simmering water. Beat with electric beaters on medium speed for 3–4 minutes or until thick. Remove the bowl from the heat and continue to beat for a further 2–3 minutes until the mixture is cool and almost double in volume. Sift the flour over the mixture and pour in the butter and vanilla essence carefully. Fold in quickly using the cut and lift action (p. 33) until just combined, about 20 folds.

Pour into prepared tin (pan), tap gently on the work surface twice to remove the excess air.

Place in a preheated oven at 180°C/350°F/gas 4 for 20 minutes or until sponge is golden and shrinks slightly from the sides of the tin (pan). Leave to stand for 5 minutes, turn on to a wire rack to cool completely.

Fill and ice (frost) the sponge (p. 13) with any flavoured buttercream you like (p. 45). Decorate the sides of the sponge with toasted flaked almonds (p. 47).
Serves 6.

*Above: Génoese. This fine-textured classic cake is iced with a simple buttercream and decorated with crushed toffee. Left: Preparation for Génoese Sponge. The eggs and sugar have been beaten in the bowl over simmering water until they have thickened and doubled in volume.*

**Using Flour.** *Unless otherwise stated in a recipe always sift flour three times before using. This assists in adding lightness to the cake mixture.*

# Celebration Cakes

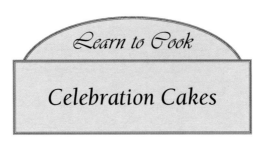

The following selection of cakes brings together all the techniques you have learned by using this book.

These are not just cakes but are in the realm of gâteaus and tortes.

Gâteau is the French word for cakes of all types; here it is featured as a rich, sometimes layered dessert cake filled with fresh whipped cream or buttercream, iced (frosted) and either simply or lavishly decorated.

Torte, on the other hand, is a German word for an open tart, or as in these recipes, a rich cake often made with ground walnuts, hazelnuts or almonds replacing some or all of the flour, and whisked eggs. You can prepare any of these special cakes in advance, to dazzle your friends when celebrating any occasion.

*Orange-Nut Torte—blended boiled oranges and ground almonds are folded into creamy-light eggs and sugar.*

# Hazelnut Praline Gâteau

*Finely ground nuts of any kind add a crunchy texture and variation of flavour to this coffee allspice sponge. You can make a praline or crushed toffee with hazelnuts to decorate the gâteau or simply fill and ice (frost) with a flavoured whipped cream and tiny raspberries or sliced berries in season.*

60 g/2 oz/½ cup hazelnuts
60 g/2 oz/½ cup self-raising (self-rising) flour
2 teaspoons instant coffee powder
1 teaspoon ground allspice

4 eggs, separated
125 g/4 oz/½ cup caster (superfine) sugar
Filling and Icing (Frosting), to decorate (p. 46)
Whole hazelnuts, to decorate

Prepare 2, 20 cm/8 inch round x 4 cm/1½ inch cake tins (pans) (p. 10).

Place hazelnuts in a blender or food processor. Blend until finely ground. Sift flour, coffee powder and allspice together on to a sheet of greaseproof (waxed) paper. Prepare sponge using Classic Method II (p. 32), adding the hazelnuts with the flour. Pour mixture evenly between prepared tins (pans). Place in the oven and bake for 15 minutes. Remove, leave to stand for 5 minutes, turn out on to a wire rack and leave to cool.

Split each sponge in half (p. 13), spread the Hazelnut Praline Filling and Icing (Frosting) as directed (p. 46). Decorate with whole hazelnuts.

*Serves 8*

# Orange-Nut Torte

2 large oranges
250 ml/8 fl oz/1 cup water
6 eggs
175 g/6 oz/¾ cup caster (superfine) sugar
200 g/7 oz/2 cups ground almonds

1 teaspoon baking powder
Icing (confectioners') sugar, to decorate
Whipped cream, to decorate
Thin orange segments, to decorate
Crystallised peel, to decorate (p. 31)

Prepare a 23 cm/9 inch spring-release tin (springform pan) (p. 10).

Wash the unpeeled oranges, place in a saucepan with the water and boil for 1½–2 hours. Cut in half and remove the pips (seeds). Place in a food processor and blend to a smooth pulp.

Place the eggs in a clean bowl and beat until creamy and thick. Beat in the sugar gradually until it dissolves. Fold in the remaining ingredients.

Pour into the prepared tin and bake in a preheated oven at 200°C/400°F/gas 6 for 50–60 minutes or until the cake shrinks slightly from the sides. Cover with a sheet of foil if it becomes too dark.

Leave to stand in the tin for 5 minutes, then release the clip and remove the sides. Leave to cool. Lift on to a serving plate. Dust with icing sugar and serve with cream and orange segments.

*Serves 8–10*

# Sacher Torte

*A rich single-layered chocolate cake originating in Vienna in the late 1800s, it is a superb finale with coffee.*

150 g/5 oz/5 squares plain (dark) chocolate, chopped
150 g/5 oz/⅔ cup butter
125 g/4 oz/½ cup caster (superfine) sugar
3 eggs, separated

125 g/4 oz/1 cup plain (all purpose) flour, sifted
2 tablespoons extra caster (superfine) sugar
200 g/7 oz/⅔ cup apricot jam (conserve)
Chocolate Ganache (p. 45)

Prepare a 20 cm/8 inch round cake tin (pan) (p. 10).

Place chocolate in a glass or metal bowl over a pan of simmering water to melt (p. 33). Lift out and leave to cool.

Cream butter and sugar together in a bowl until light and creamy. Beat in the egg yolks one at a time until well combined. Transfer the mixture to a large bowl, stir in the melted chocolate then fold in the flour. Beat the egg whites in a clean bowl until soft peaks form, beat in extra sugar gradually until dissolved and a meringue forms. Fold into the chocolate mixture, spread into the prepared tin. Place in the oven and bake for 25–30 minutes or until the cake shrinks slightly from the sides and the top is firm and springs back when lightly touched. Leave to stand for 5 minutes, turn on to a wire rack and cool.

Split the cake into two layers (p. 13), place on a wire rack over a shallow baking sheet.

Warm the jam in a small saucepan, push through a sieve (strainer) over a bowl. Spread some of the glaze over one layer then sandwich the layers together brushing all over with remaining glaze. Prepare the Chocolate Ganache. Pour it carefully over the cake starting from the centre, so it falls evenly down the sides to set. Transfer to a serving plate. Scrape up excess Chocolate Ganache while still warm and fill a piping bag (p. 14) with writing tip attached. Write Sacher Torte across the top.

*Serves 8–10*

# Double Choc Almond Torte

*It's all chocolate—a chocoholic's delight, this torte is best prepared a day or two in advance so the rum flavour develops. Wrapped, it will also store well for at least a week in the refrigerator.*

1 quantity Toasted Flaked Almonds (p. 47)
½ quantity Chocolate Ganache (p. 45),
   allow to stand to thicken

1 quantity No-fuss Chocolate Buttercream (p. 46)
Cocoa powder

Using Classic Method I, bake the Chocolate Cake variation (p. 27).

Trim the top of the cake if necessary and cut into three layers (p. 13). Spread the layers with some of the prepared Chocolate. Buttercream and sandwich together. Spread the remaining

*Sacher Torte. A chocolate lover's delight to eat with coffee or a fruit liqueur.*

buttercream around the sides of the cake only. Decorate the sides with Toasted Flaked Almonds and pour the Chocolate Ganache carefully over the top to reach the edges of the cake. Add more almonds to disguise the join between the two icings if necessary. Sift the cocoa powder lightly and carefully over the Ganache.

*Serves 8*

**Icing Sugar Stencils.** *Cut strips of greaseproof (waxed) paper about 1 cm/½ inch wide, and arrange in a pattern on top of the cake. Dust with sifted icing sugar. Carefully lift the paper off, leaving a clear pattern. Use pretty paper dollies to achieve the same look.*

# Black Forest Cake

*In this traditional Austrian Cake—known as a Schwarzwalder Kirschen Torte—layers of chocolate cake are filled with morello cherries, the juice of which is thickened with arrowroot and flavoured with cinnamon, then covered in whipped cream with a crown of chocolate curls and cherries.*

400 g/14 oz preserved black or morello cherries
125 ml/4 fl oz/½ cup reserved cherry juice
30 g/1 oz/2 tablespoons arrowroot
450 ml/¾ pint/2 cups double (heavy) cream

2 tablespoons Kirsch or Maraschino
Chocolate Curls, to decorate (p. 47)
Maraschino cherries, to decorate

Using Classic Method I, bake the Chocolate Cake variation (p. 27) and slice into three layers.

Drain the cherries. Remove the stones (pits) if necessary using a cherry stoner. Place the cherries in a small saucepan and add combined cherry juice and arrowroot. Stir until the mixture thickens and boils. Leave to cool.

Spread the cherry mixture on to the bottom layer of the cake. Whip the cream to firm peaks and flavour with 1–2 teaspoons of the Kirsch or Maraschino. Place the second layer of cake on top of the cherries, sprinkle with the remaining liqueur and cover with a layer of cream. Place the remaining layer of cake on top and cover the entire cake with a smooth, even layer of cream. Mark serving portions with a hot, wet knife. Decorate the top and sides of the cake with the prepared chocolate curls. Pipe a rosette of cream on each portion and top with a Maraschino cherry.

*Serves 8*

**Black Forest Cake**

*Slice cake through twice to make 3 layers. Assemble as follows:*

*Spread first layer with cherry mixture.*

*Sprinkle Kirsch on second layer and cover with cream. Cover third with cream.*

*Smooth cream and coat top and sides with chocolate curls.*

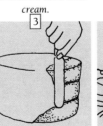
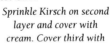

*Black Forest Cake—a superb dessert cake for a special occasion.*

# Chocolate Mocha Roulade

*Always a winner, this is a superb variation on a rolled cake method.*

125 g/4 oz/4 squares plain (dark) chocolate,
broken into pieces
2 tablespoons hot water
1 tablespoon instant coffee powder
4 eggs, separated

175 g/6 oz/¾ cup caster (superfine) sugar
1 tablespoon cocoa powder
150 ml/¼ pint/⅔ cup single (light) cream
1 teaspoon rum, brandy or any coffee liqueur

Prepare a 30 x 25 x 2.5 cm/12 x 10 x 1 inch Swiss roll tin (jellyroll pan) (p. 10).

Place the chocolate in a food processor and blend until finely chopped. Combine the water and coffee powder in a bowl, add the chocolate and stir until it has melted. Allow to cool.

Beat the egg yolks and sugar in a small bowl until very thick and pale. Add the chocolate mixture and beat together well. In a large mixing bowl, beat egg whites until stiff. Fold in chocolate mixture using a metal spoon until well combined.

Spread into the prepared pan. Bake in a preheated oven at 180°C/350°F/gas 4 for 10 minutes only. Open the oven door and leave the cake in the oven for a further 5 minutes. Dampen a clean tea-towel (dish-cloth) and place over the tin, being careful not to allow the towel to touch the cake's surface. Dust a sheet of greaseproof (waxed) paper or non-stick (bakers') parchment with the cocoa powder. When the cake is cold, turn out on to the paper.

Beat the cream in a bowl until soft peaks form, then fold in the rum, brandy or liqueur. Spread the cream carefully over the cake, roll up lightly and chill. Dust with more cocoa powder just before serving.

*Serves 6*

*Below and right: Chocolate Mocha Roulade. Dust a sheet of paper with cocoa, as illustrated, to prevent the roulade sticking as you roll it up. Chill the roulade before cutting with a sharp knife.*

# Icings, Fillings and Decorations

Some cakes stand by themselves, some require simple additions and others are elaborately filled, iced (frosted) and decorated. The icings (frostings), creams and decorative ideas that follow are suggestions for you to use. Simply check the recommendation at the base of each recipe. Once you are familiar with these recipes, add your own flavourings.

## Butter Glacé Icing (Frosting)

2 teaspoons butter
175 g/6 oz/1 cup icing (confectioners')
   sugar, sifted

1 tablespoon milk or water
A few drops of brandy, if liked

Melt the butter in a small saucepan, add the sugar, then add the milk and brandy gradually, stirring with a wooden spoon until smooth. Pour over the cake. A few drops of pink or yellow food colouring may be added.
*To cover a 20 cm/8 inch round, oblong or square cake*

## Lemon Glacé Icing (Frosting)

350 g/12 oz/2 cups icing (confectioners')
   sugar, sifted

30 g/1 oz/2 tablespoons butter, melted
6–8 teaspoons lemon juice

Combine the icing sugar, butter and sufficient lemon juice in a small bowl to form a firm paste. Stand the bowl in a pan of simmering water and stir until the icing is smooth and glossy—don't overheat or the icing will be dull and grainy.
*To cover a 20 cm/8 inch round, oblong or square cake*

## Yoghurt Icing (Frosting)

1 tablespoon plain yoghurt

90 g/3 oz/½ cup icing (confectioners') sugar, sifted

Stir both ingredients together in a bowl until smooth and well combined.
*To cover a 20 cm/8 inch round or square cake*

# Chocolate Rum Icing (Frosting)

250 g/9 oz/generous 1 cup butter
225 g/8 oz/1⅓ cups icing (confectioners')
   sugar, sifted

4–6 tablespoons rum
60 g/2 oz/½ cup plain (dark) chocolate, finely
   grated

Beat together the butter and icing sugar in small mixing bowl until light and creamy. Add the rum and chocolate, and beat until light and smooth.
*To ice (frost) and decorate a 20 cm/8 inch round cake*

# Coconut Ice Icing (Frosting)

350 g/12 oz/2 cups icing sugar, sifted
125 g/4 oz/1⅓ cups desiccated (shredded) coconut

2 egg whites, lightly beaten until foamy
Red food colouring, if liked

Mix together the icing sugar, coconut and egg white until well combined. Add food colouring, if liked.
*To cover a 20 cm/8 inch cake*

# Chocolate Ganache

175 ml/6 fl oz/¾ cup single (light) cream

250 g/9 oz/9 squares plain (dark) chocolate, finely
   chopped

Heat the cream in a small saucepan until simmering. Remove and stir in the chocolate. Leave to stand for 5 minutes, stir until the chocolate melts, then chill. Beat with a whisk or wooden spoon for 30–60 seconds until slightly thickened.
*To ice (frost) and decorate a 20 cm/8 inch cake*

# Buttercreams

275 g/10 oz/1¼ cup butter
3 eggs
3 egg yolks

225 g/8 oz/1 cup caster (superfine) sugar
1 teaspoon vanilla essence (extract)

Beat the butter until light and creamy. Place the eggs, egg yolks, sugar and vanilla essence in a bowl over a saucepan of simmering water and beat continuously until the consistency is thick and creamy. Remove from the heat and continue to beat until cool. Add the egg mixture to the butter slowly, beating continuously. Add a little at a time, making sure it is fully blended in before adding more.
*To fill and ice (frost) a 20 cm/8 inch cake*

## Making Praline

| | | | |
|---|---|---|---|
| *Simmer sugar and hazelnuts in saucepan until dissolved and golden.* | *Pour on to a greased, foil-covered flat metal sheet and leave to set.* | *Break up toffee with a knife handle.* | *Crush with rolling pin or in food processor to make a fine praline.* |

 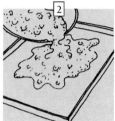  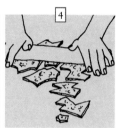

# Hazelnut Praline Filling and Icing (Frosting)

200 g/7 oz/scant 1 cup caster (superfine) sugar
60 g/2 oz/½ cup hazelnuts, chopped
350 g/12 oz/2 cups icing (confectioners')
 sugar, sifted

500 g/18 oz/1¼ cups cream cheese, softened to
 room temperature

Place the caster sugar and hazelnuts together in a heavy-based saucepan over a very low heat, without stirring for about 5–6 minutes until the sugar dissolves and turns golden. Pour immediately on to a baking sheet covered with well-greased foil and leave to set. Break up with a knife handle, then use a food processor or rolling pin to crush it to a fine praline.

Beat together the icing sugar and cream cheese until light and smooth. Reserve half for icing, and fold ½ cup praline into the remainder to make the cake filling.
*To cover and fill a 20 cm/8 inch cake*

# No-Fuss Buttercream

375 g/12 oz/1½ cups butter, softened
175 g/6 oz/2 cups icing (confectioners') sugar
 sifted

1 teaspoon vanilla essence (extract) or
1 tablespoon rum or brandy or
1 tablespoon clear honey

Beat together the butter and icing sugar until very light and creamy. Beat in the vanilla essence, rum, brandy or honey.
*To fill and ice (frost) a 20 cm/8 inch cake*

**Chocolate:** Add 2–3 tablespoons sifted cocoa powder mixed with 2 teaspoons milk with the icing sugar.

# Whipped Vanilla Cream

*600 ml/1 pint/2½ cups double (heavy) cream,*
*    well chilled*

*100 g/3½ oz/⅔ cup icing (confectioners') sugar, sifted*
*1 teaspoon vanilla essence (extract)*

Beat the cream until soft peaks form. Add the icing sugar and vanilla essence, and continue beating until firm peaks form or until the cream peaks remain upright.
*To fill and cover a 20–23 cm/8–9 inch cake*

**Coffee Cream:** Omit the vanilla and fold in 1 tablespoon finely ground fresh coffee or 2 teaspoons instant coffee powder.
**Rum or Brandy Cream:** Omit the vanilla and fold in 1–2 tablespoons rum or brandy.
**Citrus Cream:** Fold in 1 tablespoon finely grated orange rind.

# Chocolate Shavings

Take a 400 g/14 oz/4 squares plain (dark) chocolate slab and draw a vegetable peeler down one edge of the chocolate to make shavings over a sheet of non-stick (bakers') parchment.
*To cover a 23 cm/9 inch cake*

# Chocolate Curls

Pour 400 g/14 oz/14 squares melted plain (dark) chocolate on to a marble slab or cold surface and use a palette or straight edged knife to spread thinly. As the chocolate begins to set, hold a large knife at a 45° angle to the slab and pull gently through the chocolate. Work quickly or the chocolate will harden and splinter.
*To cover a 23 cm/9 inch cake*

# Toasted Flaked Almonds

Spread 250 g/9 oz/2¼ cups flaked (slivered) almonds thinly onto a baking sheet. Bake in a preheated oven at 180°C/350°F/gas 4 for 4 minutes. Remove the baking sheet and use a fork to turn the almonds. Return to the oven and bake for a further 4 minutes. Remove and turn again. Continue this until the almonds are golden brown. Allow to cool on the baking sheet. When cool, press them around the sides of a cake covered with glaze or cream.
*To cover sides of a 23 cm/9 inch cake*

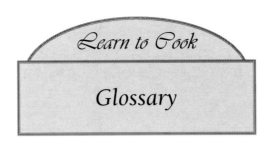

# Glossary

**Allspice:** A Caribbean spice also known as Pimento. Its flavour is similar to that of a blend of cinnamon, cloves and nutmeg.

**Chocolate:** Cooking; made basically from vegetable fat, with a low cocoa content, which melts easily.

**Essence:** Extract, concentrated liquid used for flavouring.

**Flour:** Dusting tins with flour after greasing to ease release after baking.

**Fold:** Combining aerated mixtures such as egg whites with other ingredients to maintain volume, using a cutting and lifting action. Best achieved with a metal spoon.

**Gâteau:** French term for any type of large cake, usually decorated in some way.

**Glazing:** Covering a cake with jam (jelly or conserve), sugar syrup or egg yolk to give it a shiny surface, or used to separate the cake from another layer.

**Grease:** To coat the inside of a tin with butter or oil to make it easier to remove the food after baking.

**Kirsch:** Brandy made with the fermented pulp of small black cherries, made in Switzerland.

**Meringue:** Whisked egg white that has sugar gradually added to it during its aeration.

**Mixed Fruit:** A combination of sultanas (golden raisins), raisins, currants, mixed citrus peel and cherries.

**Mixture:** A general term for a combination of ingredients, in a state prior to cooking.

**Peel:** The outside skin of citrus fruit which is grated or thinly peeled.

**Praline:** Chopped nuts, usually almonds, cooked in sugar to caramelize.

**Roulade:** Sponge roll (jelly roll)

**Sandwich:** Joining together of 2 cakes with jam, cream or icing

**Soured Cream:** A thick commercially cultured cream which has been soured.

**Syrup:** Thick solution prepared by boiling sugar and water with other flavourings being added such as orange peel.

**Whip:** Add air and increase volume

**Whisk:** Use a fork or kitchen whisk to mix in a fast circular motion to combine ingredients.